girl Talk

Staying Strong, Feeling Good, Sticking Together

by
Judith Harlan

Illustrated by Debbie Palen

Walker and Company

New York

First published in the United States of America in 1997 by Walker Publishing Company, Inc.

Published simultaneously in Canada by Thomas Allen & Son Canada, Limited, Markham, Ontario

Library of Congress Cataloging-in-Publication Data
Harlan, Judith.

Girl talk: staying strong, feeling good, sticking together/Judith Harlan; illustrations by Debbie Palen.
p.   cm.
Includes bibliographical references and index.
Summary: Offers hints, clues, and suggestions which can empower girls to shape the world into the image of their own best hopes.
ISBN 0-8027-8640-5. —ISBN 0-8027-7524-1 (pbk.)
1. Girls—Juvenile literature.   2. Preteens—Juvenile literature.   3. Self-esteem in children—Juvenile literature.   [1. Girls.   2. Self-esteem.]   I. Palen, Debbie, ill.
II. Title.
HQ777.H28   1997
305.23—dc21   97–16806
                                                                CIP
                                                                AC

Book design by Chris Welch

Printed in the United States of America
8   10   9   7

To Connie, who said,
Women are the strong ones.

contents

acknowledgments

Thanks to my editor, Mary Perrotta Rich, of Walker and Company, who was the impetus and encouragement for *Girl Talk*. And to my friends who are mothers and sent their daughters to me to assert their desires, frustrations, and hopes. And to my friends who are not mothers but remember what it was like to be girls and who enthusiastically shared their ideas. And to the girls, with special thanks to Corinne Rouse and Jacklyn Singer. And, finally, to my own mother, Ruth Harlan; sister, Jan Walters; and husband, Terry Tintorri, who encourage me always.

introduction

This book is about what every girl already knows but is in danger of forgetting as she enters the chaos of her teen years. It's about the joy of holding on to the confidence of girlhood while growing into womanhood. And it's about shaping the world at the same time, so that the world that develops around you is the world you want to live in.

It's about knowing something about our female history and getting interested in learning more about the women who came before us and helped shape our world. It's about opening doors for girls and boys, women and men.

Introduction

This is a book of clues, some of which will be meaningful for some girls, some of which will help others. All of the clues and ideas are meant for one basic purpose—to shape the world into the image of a girl's own best hopes.

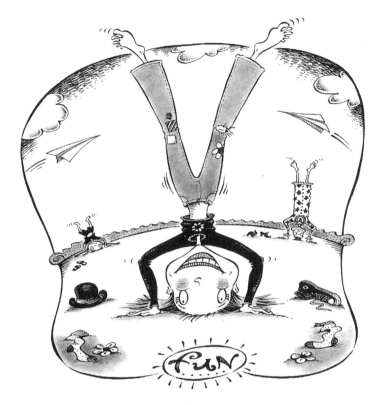

When was the last time you stood on your head and wiggled your toes at the sky? Children do things like that just because they're fun. They go rolling down hills and racing up stairs—just to be rolling and racing. And why not?

The question is, why aren't *you* doing more of it now? Sure, you risk having some people look at you funny and tell you that you're supposed to be a "young adult." They will also remind you to sit still and admonish you to be quiet.

But, honestly, don't you still sometimes have that old urge to run across an open lot with your arms stretched straight out from your sides, and your mouth wide-open and screaming, like a jet on takeoff? So go ahead. Do it. Enjoy yourself. Pretend you're a jet. Or pretend you're a snowball and roll around the yard.

These are the in-between years. Some days you'll have the urge to jump up and down like a wild woman on a pogo stick; other days you'll have the desire to sit quietly among peers and discuss world events. Why not have both?

The secret that most grown women won't let you in on is that many of them sometimes have the same urge to run like a superjet across an open field. But they don't. They remind themselves of their maturity and put on a serious face. But why?

Having fun doesn't have to end with childhood. Having fun is simply holding on to the joy of each day. It's looking up at the sky and taking a deep breath just because it feels good. It's laughing at the shapes in clouds and dancing in the rain. It's letting go of the "should" voices that tell you that you *should* settle down. It's listening, instead, to the voice inside that says, "Girl, wouldn't it be fun to stand on your head and wiggle your toes at the sky?"

The joy of being a kid, and a girl-kid at that, is one that you can hold on to forever, a joy that will enrich your life through all the years until you're a ninety-five-year-old woman who still laughs at the clouds and dances in the rain. A few suggestions for holding on to your own inner-girl joy . . .

Could she be your hero?

Whoopi Goldberg began acting when she was eight years old, as a player in the Helena Rubinstein Children's Theater. Along the way, she discovered that she was funny. She told jokes and did impressions of movie stars. Today she is a movie star herself and one of the world's best-loved comedians.

Run through sprinklers.

Make paper airplanes and fly them.

Run through the rain.

Learn how to make balloon animals (from a book in the library) and amuse the neighborhood kids—and yourself—with balloon poodles, balloon birds, and weird balloon hats.

∙∙∙

CLOWN TALK

Priscilla Mooseburger took clowning around to new heights. She joined the circus—Ringling Brothers Barnum and Bailey Circus. As a female clown, she was a trailblazer for many other women who wanted to be clowns. Today she teaches clowning to both women and men at her Mooseburger Clowning Camp. "Your clowning begins with you," she says, "how you feel about yourself and your world."

∙∙∙

Swing from a rope.

Run as fast as you can, just for fun.

OTHER WOMEN HAVE DONE IT

They laughed their way to the top! Many women have made it big in show business by telling jokes. To name a few: Ellen DeGeneres, Rosie O'Donnell, Whoopi Goldberg, Paula Poundstone, Margaret Cho, Lily Tomlin, Brett Butler, Ellen Cleghorne, Roseanne, Janeane Garofalo. So, do you know a few jokes?

Do a cannonball off the diving board.

Practice juggling tennis balls until you get really, really, really, really good at it.

Roll down a grassy hillside.

Learn how to make a "cat's cradle" with string. Sure, it's an oddball thing to do, but you might be the only kid in class who knows how to do it!

Sing in the shower.

Put on a puppet show.

Find someone making cookies and be there when they come out of the oven.

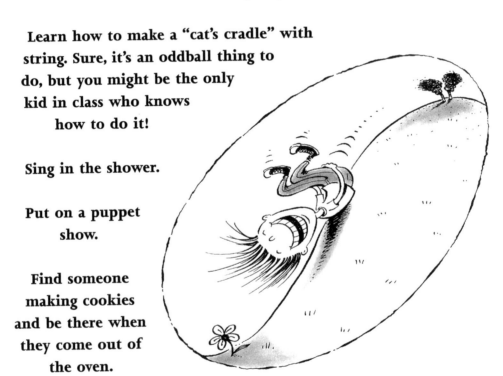

Is it autumn? Find some fallen leaves and listen to them crunch as you stomp through them.

Paint a picture.

Could she be your hero?
Christa Rypins makes a living doing two of her favorite things at the same time—juggling and ice skating. How did she get into such a fun field? First, she trained as an ice dancer. Then she taught herself to juggle with three small balls and a how-to book. Then she became a juggling ice dancer.

Hop all the way down the block.

Dance in the falling snow.

Build a snowman. And a snowwoman, a snowgirl, a snowboy, and a snowbaby. Build a whole village of snowpeople! Don't forget the snowdog.

SILENT STARS

Have you ever watched a mime pretend to be trapped in a box? Or run in slow motion? The art of mime combines dance, theater, and sometimes acrobatics. But watch closely. Often there's a deeper meaning to the mimes' movements. Mamako Yoneyama (Mamako the Mime), famous in the 1970s, used mime to tell stories of a woman searching for enlightenment.

Make hand shadows of dogs and alligators on a blank wall.

Play hackey sack all by yourself.

Turn off the television. Do something else.

It's a Fact

Medical doctors today talk about the mind and body connection and the health benefits of enjoying life. In other words, having fun can be beneficial to your health.

Pretend you're dancing in a rock video. Put your whole self into it and bow at the end.

Do a headstand and wiggle those toes!

How wonderful to be happy for no reason.
—Greta Garbo (actor)

my ideas for more fun

_____
_____
_____
_____
_____
_____
_____
_____
_____
_____
_____

In the early 1990s, an athletic shoe company had a great slogan: "Just Do It." If you like running, run. If you like speed skating, speed skate. If you see someone on television rowing a canoe, and you think, "That's what I want to do," try it out. After all, what's stopping you?

As you grow up, you receive mixed messages from the world around you. Gym teachers tell you that you should build strong muscles and a healthy body through sports and exercise. Your peers tell you that the cool girls are the cheerleaders who stay on the sidelines and root for the boys' football team. And furthermore, they say, guys don't like muscular girl-athletes. So, where does this leave you? Sure, it's a thrill to rapid-dribble a ball down a basketball court or bench-press your own weight, but is it worth social suicide?

Or is it possible that maybe, just maybe, you can have both? Maybe you can be an all-out, radical girl-jock and still be as popular as you want to be. Maybe you can run your life's races by your own rules.

Later, when you're an adult woman, you'll be considered even more attractive if you snowboard, waterski, golf, skate, run, play basketball, or enjoy any other sports. (You did know that, didn't you?) But what about now? It takes some strength of character to swim against the tide of social pressure. And that pressure is surging in, from media images of thin, no-muscle models, to parents who would like you to quiet down, to friends who are reacting to the pressures themselves. Almost everybody is beginning to expect you to settle down and sit on the sidelines.

So what are you gonna do, girl? Are you going to settle down? Or are you going to play ball? How about going out right now, enlisting a few friends as partners, and getting together for a game? How about making your own rules and enjoying your own thrill of victory and agony of defeat? How about refusing to limit yourself to the sideline as spectator? Are you ready? On your mark, get set . . .

Get up a game of in-line hockey with your girlfriends.

Take your friends to a batting cage. Have fun cheering each other when you hit the balls.

Do skateboard tricks.

Take a lifeguard course.

Play ball. Congratulate the losing team players. They played their best, and so did you. Everybody's a player, and that means everybody wins!

OTHER WOMEN HAVE DONE IT

In 1978, thirteen-year-old Penny Dean set a record for swimming the English Channel. She swam it in seven hours and forty minutes, two hours faster than the male record holder!

Pick a girl to be captain of the team during coed team sports.

Like the snow? Try snowboarding. Like the ocean? Try surfing. A female's lower center of gravity gives her an advantage in both of these sports.

. . . .

OTHER WOMEN HAVE DONE IT

Women are tough. In 1990, Susan Butcher set a new record of eleven days, one hour, fifty-three minutes, and twenty-three seconds for the Anchorage-Nome Iditarod Trail Sled Dog Race, a 1,159-mile race across the frozen rivers and tundra of Alaska.

. . . .

Make friends with a boy who is not good at sports.

Don't just watch, do. And bring your own sense of fairness to the game. A strongly competitive game does not have to mean that someone goes home feeling like a loser.

Could she be your hero? In 1991, jockey Julie Krone broke through the barriers against women jockeys in high-stakes horse racing and rode in the Belmont Stakes. In 1993, she rode in it again and won!

Go out and cheer the girls' running team with as much enthusiasm as you cheer the boys' teams.

Join a soccer team. Or baseball. Or basketball. Or swimming. Or the sport of your choice.

How about that basketball hoop in the driveway or down the street? Do you girls ever use it? Would you like to? Go ahead. If it's public property, you are as much the public as the guys are.

Little-Known History

You've heard of bullfights. And maybe you've heard of the annual ritual in Pamplona, Spain, where men run through the streets, chased by bulls? Well, legend has it that in ancient Crete women ran *at* charging bulls, grabbed their horns, and then *jumped over them!*

Is dancing your sport? Join a ballet troupe or a jazz dancing group. Or start one of your own.

Oh Yeah???

A boy comes up to you while you're playing baseball. He says, "You throw like a girl."

You say, "Just like Jackie Mitchell! Thanks!" Because you and your girlfriends know the inside story: Jackie Mitchell (a female!!) struck out Babe Ruth and Lou Gehrig, two of America's most famous baseball hitters, in a 1931 exhibition game.

Start your own bicycle club for girls. Get together with your girlfriends, help each other with bicycle maintenance, and go for rides and races together.

Hmmm . . .

National Football League players need to be big, and men, on average, are bigger than women. So we all agree that it's logical for NFL football players to be male.

Horse racing jockeys need to be small, and women, on average, are smaller than men. Yet most jockeys are male. Is there a failure of logic here?

Recall how many times you've watched boys play casual, neighbor-hood games of basketball, hockey, and football. Now recall how many times boys have stood around and seriously watched girls play sports. The next time you find yourself sitting on the side-lines watching boys play a game, get up and do something else.

Instead of choosing up sides as "boys against girls," mix the teams up. Have fun, without having to prove anything.

It's a Fact

In 1995, Kelly Robbins earned $180,000 for working a few days at a job she loves—playing golf. (She won the 1995 championship!)

Watch your local television sports news and expect to see women's college sports covered (if men's college sports are). If women's sports are not covered, call the station and say you want to know the day's scores for women's sports teams.

Could she be your hero?

Lisa Leslie didn't start playing basketball until she was in the seventh grade. She discovered she was good at it and kept playing on girls' and boys' teams. In 1996, she was a star on the women's U.S. Olympic basketball team and was photographed for Vogue magazine, as well as Sports Illustrated.

Look out your window and notice the kids (and adults) on your street playing games—flying kites, riding bikes, skimming by on skateboards or snowsleds, throwing balls or Frisbees—and get out there and do something yourself.

Pay attention in gym class.

Follow your dreams and always remember to go for it!
—Billie Jean King (Director, World Team Tennis)

my ideas for more active sports

_____

_____

_____

_____

_____

_____

_____

_____

_____

_____

_____

fashion

If you're going to be stylish, you must have the right look. All the fashion magazines tell you so. They also eventually get around to telling you that you must find YOUR look. That look must express you, the individual, the one and only, the *independent* you—independent as long as you don't break any of this season's fashion rules.

Following these style rules doesn't sound like fun, but it can be. It's fun to get dressed in the latest, coolest styles and see how they feel. It's fun to try out jewelry and makeup and shoes and sunglasses. It's fun to get together with girlfriends and paint your toenails in polka dots. And it's especially fun to throw on those clothes that make your mother shudder.

Still, the negative side to the fashion issue is always there. Fashion is pressure. It dictates to you what you *should* be wearing, and how you *must* look to be acceptable. Magazines are full of rules on achieving the perfect *body*, the perfect *face*, the perfect *hair*. And the message is clear: Girls *must* be fashionably perfect to be popular.

Another message is that to be fashionable, girls must look like the bony, X-ray models in the magazines. That's pressure! Today's models weigh about 23 percent less than the normal, average woman! Girls put pressure on each other, too, by judging the girls in their school according to how they dress, and by expecting all the girls in their social group to dress alike.

But you are different, remember, an individual—and determined to stay in charge of your own life. Here are two key questions to keep you on top of fashion, not under it: (1) What does fashion really mean to you? And (2) what do you want it to mean? And now, some inside fashion clues for the independent thinker . . .

Read the fashion "dos and don'ts" in your favorite magazine. Then do whatever you please.

- -

H O W   F A R ?

How far will you go to fit in?
- ○ Shoes that pinch. Ouch!
- ○ Waist nippers and body shapers (girdles in disguise) that squeeze. Gasp!
- ○ Bras that push. Oomph.
- ○ Diets that starve or even endanger your health!
- ○ Piercing—"Everybody's doing it."
- ○ Tattoos—permanent ink stains!
- ○ Anything the crowd says is cool.

- -

Wear something today just because you like it, not because it matches, it's stylish, or your friends like it.

The next time you find yourself tugging at your clothes to keep them from riding up or falling off, change clothes.

Go to your closet. Pull out your favorite outfit. Next, pull out your most comfortable outfit. If they are one and the same, congratulations. If not, why not?

Look in a full-length mirror. Are you tall? Terrific! Short? Celebrate! Medium? Wonderful. Women come in all sizes, and all sizes are beautiful.

Spend time shaping your LIFE, not your body.

Hmmm . . .

Fashion is not just clothes-deep. In the 1950s, the Marilyn Monroe look
was a hit, so women gained weight to fit the image. In the 1960s, the
stick-thin, boyish, Twiggy look was the groovy thing, so women lost
weight—lots of it. In the 1990s, magazines still feature bone-thin
women, but the gyms are full of women building muscles. Are women
today beginning to make their own body rules? Are you?

1950   1966   1998

Look in a mirror. Pose as if you are the president of the United States. Still being the president, walk across the room. Notice how you are walking. Do you look more confident now? Do you like the look?

Clock how much time you spend combing your hair, applying makeup, and getting dressed. Then spend an equal amount of time DOING something FUN, like skating, riding a bike, playing the saxophone, or designing your own fashions.

....

OTHER WOMEN HAVE DONE IT

Annie Leibovitz, one of today's top photographers, didn't have much professional experience when she walked into *Rolling Stone* magazine's editorial offices in 1970, but she had a collection of photos she had taken in her photo classes. The editor sent her out to photograph John Lennon, a member of the Beatles rock group. Since then, Leibovitz has photographed many famous people, such as Whoopi Goldberg, Dolly Parton, and supermodel Lauren Hutton. In fact, she is as rich and famous now as many of the people she photographs.

....

Are you feeling the need to shave? In much of the world, women don't shave armpits and legs. In the United States, most women do. Shaving is not a biological necessity. It's a decision. Decide for yourself.

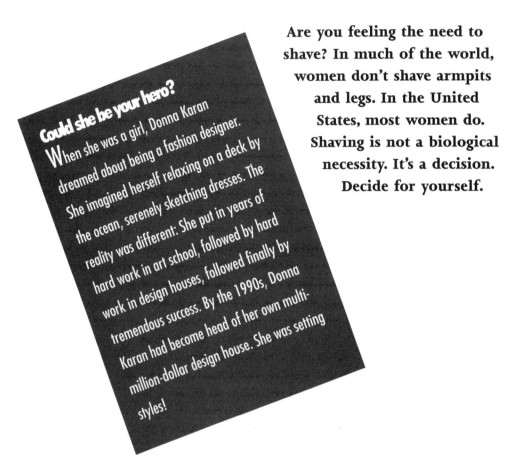

Could she be your hero?

When she was a girl, Donna Karan dreamed about being a fashion designer. She imagined herself relaxing on a deck by the ocean, serenely sketching dresses. The reality was different: She put in years of hard work in art school, followed by hard work in design houses, followed finally by tremendous success. By the 1990s, Donna Karan had become head of her own multi-million-dollar design house. She was setting styles!

If your friends laugh at what you wear, laugh with them. And wear it anyway.

Little-Known History

In the fourth century, pants were considered "unmanly" and worn only by women in Western society. Then fashions changed, and women turned to skirts and gave the pants to men. Pants became the "manly" style. The separation of styles became so rigid that in 1850 American men threw rocks at women who wore bloomers (loose trousers worn under skirts) in public. Now Western women wear pants freely once again. And men? Would you let them wear skirts? Or would you throw rocks at them?

Tell a wrinkled old woman she's beautiful. Because—look closely—she is. She has a lifetime of smiles and tears and wisdom on her face.

Look in a mirror. Find both of your parents in your own face.

Hmmm . . .

In China, for centuries all beautiful women had the "lotus foot." To achieve this three-inch, clawlike foot, mothers wrapped their daughters' feet so tightly from the age of four that the bones were crushed into deformed stumps. Lotus foot ladies were usually carried because when they walked, they hobbled in pain. Men worshiped them for this helpless "beauty." Today things have changed. Foot binding is long gone. Yet all over the world, men love to see women wobbling carefully, often painfully, along in pointed-toe, high-heeled shoes. Of course, it's not the same thing. Or is it?

The next time you go to a wedding, notice how many women kick off their shoes before the dancing's done; now notice how many men are shoeless.

Coco Chanel

Check out a library book on fashion history. Read about the famous women in fashion who were not models— Coco Chanel, Anne Klein, Liz Claiborne, Norma Kamali, Laura Ashley, Betsey Johnson, Bonnie Cashin, Rei Kawakubo, the Fendi women, Diane Von Fürstenberg, and Donna Karan— women who designed beautiful clothes for other women.

Diane Von Fürstenberg

Schedule a day with your girlfriends when you each wear one color of the rainbow: red, orange, yellow, green, blue, indigo, and violet. Be a rainbow of friends.

Trade heritages with a friend for a day. You wear something that comes from her culture. She wears something from yours.

You will always be in fashion if you are true to yourself, and only if you are true to yourself.

—Maya Angelou (writer)

my fashion dos and don'ts

_____

_____

_____

_____

_____

_____

_____

_____

_____

_____

_____

Girlfriends

What's going on with your girlfriends lately? Are they settling in to watch boys play games more than they're playing games themselves? Are they talking more about their hair than about the latest in-line skates? Are they focusing on boys? Are some of them even starting to lose confidence and say things like "I don't know" more than ever before? Are you? And are you getting just a bit bored with it all? If so, it's time to start shaking things up.

It's time to take charge. It's time to find your balance between what you want to be and what your girlfriends want you to be.

If you notice that you're having more fun than ever with your friends and laughing more than ever before, great! You have a hundred new mysteries, like dating, that you and your girlfriends are all figuring out together. But if you find that you are talking and sitting more than actually *doing* anything lately—not so great. That means the balance of your life is shifting.

Finding your own center of balance with your girlfriends in these shifting times takes some thought. You have to ask yourself: How do you want to shape your own life and your friendships? How are you going to make sure that you are running your own life and not being run by others? ("Peer pressure"?) And how will you combine your life with the lives of your friends?

These are tough questions to ponder. But now is the time to ponder them, to put some thought into your own personal vision of life. What's your view of what's fun, right, and meaningful? What do *you* want to be doing? Truly, managing your life and friendships is a balancing act. Sometimes you feel as if you're walking a tightrope and your friends are doing their best to pull you off balance. Sometimes you feel that you could balance on the tip of a flagpole and boost your friends up beside you without losing your foothold, you're that sure of yourself.

Always, you are aware of how important your girlfriends are in shaping your life. And you know you are all changing. As your personalities mature, this is the time to take charge and plan some inspiring events—events that excite you as well as your girlfriends.

Have a Super Bowl party—just for the girls. And do whatever you please during the game.

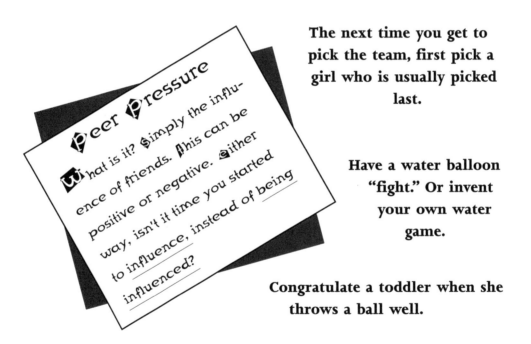

Peer Pressure

What is it? Simply the influence of friends. This can be positive or negative. Either way, isn't it time you started to influence, instead of being influenced?

The next time you get to pick the team, first pick a girl who is usually picked last.

Have a water balloon "fight." Or invent your own water game.

Congratulate a toddler when she throws a ball well.

Little-Known History

Does pink look like a girls' color to you? Before 1920, it wasn't. Then both girls and boys under six wore mostly white. In the 1920s, pink became the boys' color, and blue was the girls' color. About fifteen years later, the colors switched, and pink became the girls' color. Maybe it's time for another switch. Or even for an end to separate colors for girls and boys.

Look at your girlfriends. Are you all wearing similar styles? Why? Or, why not?

....

OTHER WOMEN HAVE DONE IT

A group of Brooklyn fifth-grade girls made the news in 1993 when they built a six-foot-long suspension bridge out of Erector sets. The girls were members of their school's Civil Engineering Club, and their project won first prize in the school division of the Erector Set Contest.

....

Always keep a secret.

Make a video with your girlfriends.

Could she be your hero?

Jodie Foster gained early fame as an actor, but she has since gained even more as a director, at the helm of such movies as Little Man Tate and Home for the Holidays.

Jodie Foster

Have a soirée (a sharing party). Have each girl show what she does best: for example, play the guitar, read a poem she wrote, give her opinion on a political event, perform gymnastics.

Hold a car wash to raise funds for a local charity. Or a pet wash.

Are you on a sports team? Invite your girlfriends to come to your games (or meets) and cheer you on.

Girlpower —IT'S A FACT!

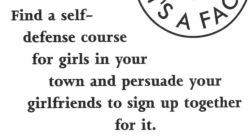

HII-YAA!

Find a self-defense course for girls in your town and persuade your girlfriends to sign up together for it.

Get together with a couple of girlfriends and lots of magazines. Working separately, cut out images that reflect your most perfect dream life, and make your own collage. Now compare all the collages. Do you see differences? Similarities?

Little-Known History

Sarah and Angelina Grimké were sisters from South Carolina. They joined forces to speak out against slavery in the 1830s, and they attracted thousands to their antislavery lectures. But they also attracted anger from many sides. People at the time believed that it was indecent of women to give speeches in public. They ridiculed and harassed the Grimké sisters and called them "unnatural." Before long, Sarah and Angelina not only were speaking out for an end to slavery but were arguing in public for women's rights, too!

Sarah Grimké

Angelina Grimké

Make friends with a lonely girl.

Be happy for your girlfriends when they do well.

Like music? Learn to play the guitar, the drums, the bass guitar, the saxophone, the keyboard. Start your own band.

Take your music group on the road. Perform for neighbors and friends and school assemblies.

MUSICAL NOTES

Fender Guitar, the preferred electric guitar for bands, named a guitar after Bonnie Raitt. She's a rock star famous for her brilliant slide guitar and vocals, and she has also helped raise thousands of dollars for programs to encourage girls to learn electric guitar.

Hmmm . . .

Experts say that females' friendships with each other are some of the deepest and richest of all. Often, these friendships last a lifetime, through schools, colleges, marriages, and the births of children. Yet when a guy finds out a girl is "just" planning to spend time with her girlfriends on Saturday night, he will often pressure her to reschedule and go out with him instead.

Language Clues

Did you know that in the 19th Century, when a woman took a job as a doctor, she was called a doctress, and if she was a poet, she was called a poetess? A female professor was a professoress. And a female priest was a priestess. A woman might be an authoress, a sorceress, a tailoress, a waitress—OOPS. We still have waitresses, and come to think of it, actresses, too. Will these words sound just as silly one day as "poetess" and "doctress" sound today?

Is there something you'd like to try, but it's still considered "boys' territory"? (For example, trying out for some sports teams or entering some contests?) Enlist a girlfriend or two to go with you to the tryout or contest to be your support team.

Write a weekly newsletter about all the great things the girls in your circle have done that week. Give them space in the newsletter to voice their opinions and tell their jokes.

Get on the Internet and find other girls on the Internet who want to change things, too. Or create a homepage of your own.

Together with a girlfriend explore computers. Try some computer art projects, some on-line surfing, some computer games, and try creating some programs of your own.

Keep a journal or scrapbook to record all the highlights of these years.

Speak up and speak out—women are shy about speaking. My motto is say it—say it again only louder and with more firmness and then say it again with a smile but don't flinch.
—Barbara A. Mikulski (U.S. senator, Maryland)

my own new plans for my girlfriends and me

Guys 'n' Buds

Remember when boys were just pals, people and friends you could play ball with, run through the backyard with, do cannonballs into the pool with? Before you noticed real differences between them and you?

Now that you've noticed those differences, isn't it tempting to "choose up sides" and get into some real down-and-dirty male bashing? It's so easy. There are the jokes. (Question: "What are the three longest years in a boy's life?" Answer: "Eighth grade.") And there are the eye-rolling and immediately satisfying comments such as, "He'll never understand; he's a *male!*"

But boys are people too, and they are just as clueless during their young teen years as anyone. So instead of focusing on how different guys are and how impossible they are to get along with, let's look at some ways they are not so different.

Boys, like girls, usually like to get outdoors and aimlessly run and climb and bike and skate and play ball games. They are changing physically and emotionally. Like girls, they now have more responsibility at home and are expected to be more serious in school. They are energetic and self-conscious. They have peer pressures as well as confusion about what roles they are expected to play.

They probably sound a lot like you and your girlfriends. And they are, but they are different in that they have one great fear that girls do not have: They are afraid to admit any confusions or fears. And at the same time, they've somehow gotten the impression that they are superior.

No matter how great they think they are, though, boys are limited by the narrow roles they believe they are allowed to play. Girls' lives are limited in similar ways. So wouldn't it be terrific for both guys and girls to relate to each other in an honest way, without roles, and without stereo-types? Not an easy task, but it can be done. Here are a few ideas to get you started.

The next time someone needs a baby-sitter, ask a boy to do the job.

Trade household chores for two weeks with your brother.

Teach a boy to dance.

Hmmm . . .

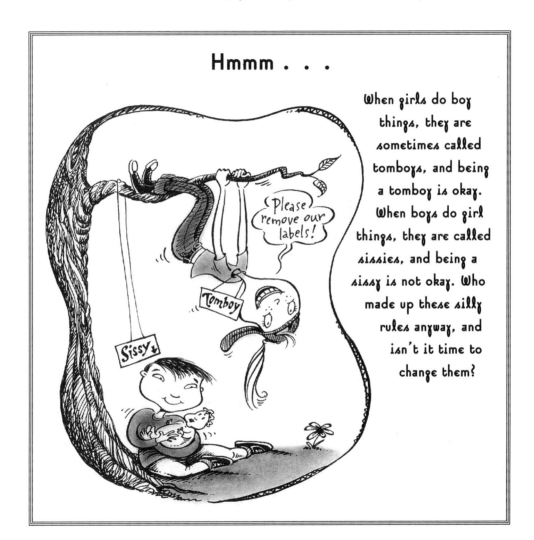

When girls do boy things, they are sometimes called tomboys, and being a tomboy is okay. When boys do girl things, they are called sissies, and being a sissy is not okay. Who made up these silly rules anyway, and isn't it time to change them?

Congratulate a boy when he does something that is a "girls' thing" and does it well.

Try something you're curious about, but you're afraid to do because it's boys' territory. Like changing a bicycle tire, troubleshooting your computer for problems, or building a science project. Don't quit if you don't do it well. No one does the first time.

Are you afraid guys won't like you if you're in charge? Learn this phrase to say to boys who object to your leadership: "Get over it."

The next time you are struggling to do something difficult and a well-meaning male— teacher, relative, or friend—tries to do it for you, say, "No. I want to do it myself. Teach me, but don't do it for me."

Could he be your hero?

When his daughter was four, Gregory Hines, a dancer, film actor, and father, suddenly realized that if his girl had been a boy, he would have already been playing ball with her. His daughter had missed at least two years of physical training. So he started playing catch with her—immediately.

Buy a doll for a baby boy. Dolls help girls develop parenting skills; boys need these skills too.

Be sincerely impressed when a boy is good at ballet. Just as you would be if he were a girl.

Don't laugh at a boy's joke if it's not funny.

- -

C R I S I S   C O N T R O L

What do you do about harassment? Some girls report that boys harass them, grab them, and insult them. And they don't know what to do. Here's what:

○ Talk to a friend.

○ Keep a detailed record of words, actions, and witnesses.

○ Tell the boy (or man) harassing you that you don't like it. Talk to him firmly, calmly, and seriously. Do not smile.

○ Also, tell an adult *exactly* what the boy said and what he did. If the first adult you tell doesn't help you, tell another one, and another one, until you find one who can make the boy stop.

○ Never think it's your fault; it isn't. Never think you asked for it; you didn't. Never think you deserve it; you don't. Walk proudly.

- -

If a guy lets you take a second shot because you missed the first time, say "no thanks."

In classroom group projects, pick a boy to be the one to take notes. Pick a girl to be the leader.

When someone tells a dumb-blond or a dumb-girl joke, don't laugh.

Could she be your hero?

In 1989, Julie Croteau became the first woman to play college baseball. Before she came along, the teams were all-male and females were forbidden to play. Croteau says that she owes a lot to the young girls who fought to play on Little League teams when they were boys-only teams in the 1970s. If not for those trailblazing girls, Croteau would not have been allowed to play Little League baseball, and that's where she developed her outstanding baseball skills. So maybe she paid those girls back by being a trailblazer herself and making it possible for women today to play college baseball.

Invite a friend who is a boy to bake cookies—and give him some *real* tasks to do, so he too can discover the fun of baking.

A Wise Day in History

When Golda Meir was prime minister of Israel (1969–1974) there was a wave of crimes against women. Golda Meir's council asked her to put a curfew on women to keep them indoors at night. She said no. If men are the problem, she said, let the council put a curfew on men.

Let the guys worry about their own egos.

When you hear a boy belittled because he is feeling sad or is sensitive, stand up for him. Say, "He has a right to his feelings." (Stand up for a girl in such a situation, too.)

Never play dumb to get a guy.

Think about this: Boys are people, too.

When you hear yourself saying, "Boys are sloppy" ("stupid," "gross," or whatever), STOP. That's stereotyping.

Let a boy cry when he needs to.

A boy of quality is not threatened by a girl for equality.

OTHER WOMEN HAVE DONE IT

In 1996, two girls won the California high school auto mechanics contest, the first girls ever to win this traditionally all-boy contest. The two-girl team competed against students from all over the state. They diagnosed engine problems, installed parts, repaired parts, and got their auto purring. They were tough; they were smart; but they were not just "one of the boys." They were girls.

Tell a guy to make his own sandwich.

Never use the word "girl" as an insult.

The sooner little boys begin to realize that little girls are equal and that there will be many opportunities for a boy to be bested by a girl, the closer they will be to better mental health.
—Sylvia Pressler (hearing officer, ruling on the integration of Little League baseball, 1973)

my own changes and plans

_____

_____

_____

_____

_____

_____

It's another day in the classroom, and maybe this is a good day because you have your homework with you and you even studied for today's quiz. Or maybe not. Either way, you are in a familiar seat in a familiar room, listening to a familiar teacher talk. So stifle that yawn and take a minute to look around you. Notice the posters on the walls. Are there any pictures of people? How many are female? How many are male?

Open your history or social studies textbook. Notice how much of it is about males and how much about females. Open your literature book and notice how many authors included there are female. Are you finding that half of the books are about or by women? Women are, after all, more than half of the population of the planet. So how do we rate in your textbooks? Do we get 50 percent of the attention? We should.

And how do we rate in your class discussions? Most teachers today try to make the classroom an inspiring place for both boys *and* girls. One of the ways they do that is by including both in their lectures and discussions. But, to be quite honest, few teachers succeed in fully including females.

They can't really make the needed changes on their own. They need the help of textbook writers, of educational sources that provide posters and materials for the classroom, and of school principals. But most of all, they need your help. They need you to speak up and insist on an equal part in class discussions and activities. And if you do, you will make your classroom into a room of your own.

Simply by speaking up, joining in, and taking a leadership role in class, you change the atmosphere in class for everyone. It's a change for the better because a class where everyone gets a chance to speak as well as listen quickly becomes an exciting, active classroom. So start by saying, "We're taking our place in the classroom," and then . . .

Learn to use the microscope (and other science equipment) by yourself.

Learn how to operate and program the school's computers.

**Start a buddy program with your friends. When one girl
is being harassed by other students, take turns
being her buddy until the
harassment stops.**

GENDER BIAS —
LEARN TO RECOGNIZE IT

Do you have a teacher who:

❑ Calls on boys more than girls?

❑ Spends more time responding to ideas from boys during discussion than to similar ideas from girls?

❑ Tends to help boys struggle through an answer until they get it, but tends to just tell girls the answer?

❑ Tends to congratulate boys on their answers more than girls?

❑ Allows boys to operate and dominate computer and science lab equipment while girls stand by and watch?

❑ Allows most of the school grounds to be used by boys for ball games, leaving girls no room for active games?

❑ Excuses his/her bias by saying boys are just naturally more talkative, active, and aggressive?

If you checked any of these boxes, you have a gender-biased teacher.

If you think a teacher is gender-biased, talk to her/him privately and explain your concerns. If nothing changes, talk to your parents; if nothing changes, talk to your counselor; if nothing changes, talk to the principal; if nothing changes, talk to your friends and have them sign a petition; present that to your principal.

Sign up for an elective, advanced
math class.

Promise yourself that you will
raise your hand and volunteer at
least once a day in each class.
Then do it.

When a teacher calls for "a big,
strong boy" to help get a box off a
shelf, volunteer. Get a girlfriend
to help you if you
need help.

Earn the highest grade in your
algebra class.

Science Class

Did you ever read about how male elks battle it out over who gets to be in charge of a "harem" of female elk? Here's another way of looking at the same facts:

Female elks travel together, usually in groups of twelve, sometimes in herds of up to sixty. They graze together and give birth to young elk in the spring. The newborns grow through the summer as the females graze from place to place.

A male serves the herd. His job is to father the babies and to guard against wolves and mountain lions. The females require a strong male for this job, and each autumn new males approach the herd of females, applying for the job of bodyguard and the privilege of traveling with the herd. The females hire the winner of a fight between the male elks.

And now, how about the rest of the wild kingdom? Maybe it's time to rewrite our wild animal stories.

Ask your art teacher about Mary Cassatt, Frida Kahlo, and Judy Chicago. Ask your history teacher about Abigail Adams, Elizabeth Cady Stanton, Margaret Sanger, and Charlotte Perkins Gilman. Ask your science teacher about Rachel Carson, Barbara McClintock, and Rosalyn Yalow. Learn about the women who came before you. And bring them up in class.

Margaret Sanger   Rachel Carson

Find a teacher you respect and ask her or him to be your mentor. A mentor is like a wise big sister—someone to advise you on how to succeed in school, both academically and socially. She's on your side, to congratulate and to help. But mostly, a mentor is a friend who knows the ropes and will show you how to climb them.

It's a girl's Math secret weapon

Could she be your hero?

Mary McLeod Bethune (1875–1955) started her school for African-American girls in 1904 with so little money that the girls used burned bits of charred wood as pencils. But Bethune's school flourished, and the girls learned. In 1923, the school merged with a boys' school to become Bethune-Cookman College. And Mary McLeod Bethune continued to be influential. She helped start the National Council of Negro Women, and she was appointed by Franklin Delano Roosevelt to direct youth programs during his presidency.

The next time a teacher is boring you to death, think of a question about the subject that interests you and ask it. This trick just might turn a boring lecture into a thrilling discussion.

If a teacher tells you that you are demanding, good for you. You are demanding your equal space in the classroom.

- -

START A SUPPORT GROUP

⟳ Choose a few friends who care about doing well in school.

⟳ Meet and decide on a plan of action.

⟳ Discuss how the others can help you with your studies and how you can help them with theirs.

⟳ Set a weekly or twice-weekly meeting date at someone's house or in a school or library study area.

⟳ Start each meeting by sharing with each other how everyone helped that week or can help in the week to come.

⟳ During the meeting, work as a group or with partners on your studies.

⟳ Congratulate a member when she does well.

⟳ Keep the group open to new members. Expect some old members to drop out and some new ones to join.

- -

When the other kids in class are laughing (or groaning) at a student's wrong answer, don't join in. You hate it when it happens to you; why do it to others?

Does a traditionally "male" class interest you? Sign up for it. Persuade some of your girlfriends to sign up, too.

Little-Known History

○ In the 1700s, universities were closed to women.

○ By the late 1800s, women were still allowed into just a few universities.

○ From 1900 to 1970, though state universities opened to women, many top private universities and military academies kept their doors closed. Also, many coed universities put a limit on the number of females they would allow into their schools each year; other schools limited the number by requiring female applicants to have higher test scores than males!

○ Today, finally, most of the limits are gone; women are students in virtually all universities.

But isn't it amazing that even when education was denied to so many women for so many centuries, some women succeeded anyway and became scientists and doctors and educators and leaders?

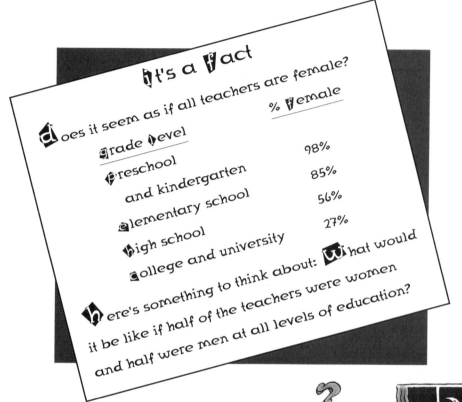

It's a Fact

Does it seem as if all teachers are female?

Grade Level	% Female
Preschool and kindergarten	98%
Elementary school	85%
High school	56%
College and university	27%

Here's something to think about: What would it be like if half of the teachers were women and half were men at all levels of education?

Help a girl with her homework.

**If the boys are hogging the computers in your school, demand
equal time for yourself and your girlfriends.**

Make it your school, too.

When I look into the future, it's so bright it burns my eyes.
—Oprah Winfrey

my own school-savvy hints

_____

_____

_____

_____

_____

_____

_____

Maybe you know what you want to be when you get older. Maybe you don't. Either way, you've reached that magic age when adults expect you to have a serious answer when they lean down, get really close to your face, and ask, "What do you want to be when you grow up?"

What's a good answer to a question like that?! You need to know not only what you *want* to be but also what you *can* be.

If you look at the job world today, you'll find that the career possibilities facing you are endless—as endless as you allow them to be. Doors to all colleges and top universities and to all careers are open to women. You know you can be anything that you want to be. So you pick a career—say, aerospace engineer—and go for it.

But wait. As you keep looking, you discover another fact about the world around you. This one is more subtle. Have you noticed it? Have you noticed that some jobs even today are considered "male" jobs and some "female"? That when most people refer to a secretary, they automatically say "she" (even though men are secretaries too), and that when people talk of an engineer, they say "he" (even though women are engineers too)?

And does it strike you as odd that most computer millionaires you see are male? And that most music and movie producers are male? And that

Civil Engineer   *Domestic Engineer*

most of the world's politicians are male? And that even most administrators of women's college sports teams are male?

The message the world is sending you—even now at the beginning of a new millennium—is that some jobs are female jobs and some are male jobs. But the message is Bunk! Hooey! Poppycock! Horsefeathers! And (*insert your own word here*).

The message is powerful only because it is delivered to you in many subtle ways, many times, every day of every week. So close your ears to this old-fashioned male-versus-female message, and keep your eyes open for the work goals that will be fulfilling to you, personally. If you want to be a truck driver, be one. Or a physicist or a police officer or a football coach!

Keep in mind that today all careers *are* open to you, and the careers where you find only a few women today will have many women tomorrow. After all, you'll be there.

Say you want to be
   a movie director, not an actor;
   a photographer, not a fashion model;
   a corporate president, not a
      secretary.
Say you want to be in charge of your
   own life.

It's a Fact

Today, women's work is work in any field they choose.

Profession	How many are women?
Business executives	45%
Engineers	8.5%
Lawyers	31%
Physicians	23%
State legislators	21.5%
U.S. congressional representatives	11.7%
U.S. senators	9%

Do you secretly want to be an astronaut, but you know everyone will laugh at you if you tell them? Read about astronauts; become an expert on astronauts' lives; study math and science and the stars. Eventually, people will HAVE to take you seriously. You'll be wearing a space suit.

Consider this job for yourself: president of the United States of America.

- -

P O P   Q U I Z

1. Who is Mary Robinson?
2. Who is Gro Harlem Brüntland?
3. Who is Benazir Bhutto?
4. Who are Sirimavo Bandaranaike and Chandrika Kumaratunga?

Clue: They all have led their countries!

[Answers: (1) president of Ireland; (2) prime minister of Norway; (3) prime minister of Pakistan; (4) prime minister of Sri Lanka and president of Sri Lanka

- -

The next time people tell you that you can't do something because you're a girl, ask them why. And keep asking until you get an answer. Then remember: They're wrong.

Get on the computer and become a bigtime computer expert!

When someone calls you bossy, say, "Thank you, I'm in training to be a CEO (chief executive officer)."

If someone tells you that you are awfully arrogant for a girl, congratulations! You are learning to trust your own opinions!

Could she be your hero? U.S. Navy officer Grace Murray Hopper invented a computer translation program in the early 1950s. This was a significant invention in computer history—it made today's user-friendly computer programs possible.

OTHER WOMEN HAVE DONE IT

Mattel, Inc., home to the Barbie doll, is not just a toy company. It is a $3.6-billion corporation. That puts it on the elite list of the top 1,000 corporations in the United States. And its top executive (its chief executive officer) as of 1997? A woman, Jill Elikann Barad.

Keep your options open by keeping your eyes open during math and science classes.

- -

START MAKING YOUR OWN MONEY TODAY

Besides the usual baby-sitting jobs, try some
    of these:

❑ Wash and wax cars.

❑ Shovel snow, mow lawns, weed gardens,
    rake leaves, wash windows.

❑ Paint garage doors or hire yourself out as
    assistant painter to neighbors.

❑ Repair bikes.

❑ Hold a neighborhood garage sale (and charge
    a percentage of sales for your efforts).

- -

Future Facts

In the 1993-94 school year, more than 35 percent of the students in college architecture and related programs were female. So, one day many architects will be women. What about you? Ever thought of being an architect? Or a surgeon? Or a truck driver? Or an engineer? Biologist? Auto mechanic? Attorney? Dentist? Chef? Detective? Senator? If there's a career that interests you, there's a path to it. Find it. Follow it.

Go to work with a woman on Take Our Daughters To Work Day. It's the fourth Thursday in April.

Do you have access to a computer? Use it.

Set your goals high and work to achieve them—and never be afraid of failure,
for the tragedy comes not in failing, but in never having tried to excel.
—Rosalynn Carter (feminist, supporter of the Equal Rights Amendment for
women, and first lady of the United States from 1977 to 1981)

my ideas for my career

_____

_____

_____

_____

_____

_____

_____

_____

_____

_____

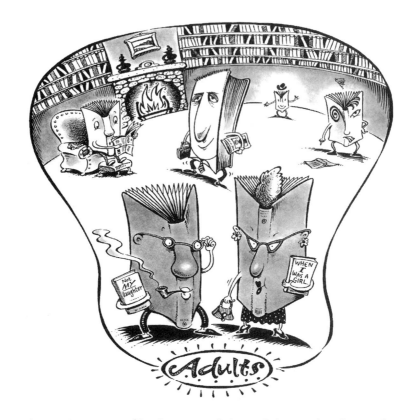

Here's another way of looking at adults. Adults are books. And a roomful of adults—that's a library. Some adults are dry, boring encyclopedias of information you'd like to avoid. Some are how-to manuals, and every time you open that book it's "do this this way" and "do that that way."

Some are hilarious comedies; you look forward to opening these books because you know they'll make you laugh. Some are wise and serious philosophy tomes: They make you think. Some are cozy bedtime stories, auto repair manuals, or recipe books. Some are short stories; some long. Some are modern novels, and some are antique poetry. And they are all around you, these walking, talking volumes. What are you going to do with them?

You can't read them all, but you can grab a little information from that old encyclopedia, learn a few basics from the repair manual, get some tender support when needed from the cozy storybook, and some inspiration from the poetry. In short, you can interact with the adults around you, learn from them, get support from them, and enjoy the warmth of building friend and family ties with them—while still remaining true to yourself.

Many teens disconnect with their families and other adults, finding them too frustrating and out of date to deal with. (Even adults admit that dealing with adults can be frustrating.) Many of them are dusty, brittle, old volumes bound tightly in ancient traditions and ladylike conventions.

The trick is to read these old books like you read your favorite novels. Listen to the stories and heed the warnings. Find the wisdom stored in these old pages. Then become the author of your own book, one that shapes your world according to your own vision.

Ask your grandparents what girls your age did when they were young.

Listen to your mother's opinions on politics with as much attention as you listen to your father's.

Shovel the snow.

Learn how one appliance in your house works.

Hmmm . . .

Insurance companies tell us that women are safer and more cautious drivers than men. Yet when a couple is in a car, note who is driving.

Take your mom fishing.

Borrow the family camera. Take pictures.

Turn on some rock music and dance around the living room with your mom.

𝕷ittle-𝕶nown𝕳istory

In ancient times in parts of Europe and around the Mediterranean Sea, the family name and the family property were passed down through the females. In those times, about 7,000 years ago, women also occupied the most respected places in their communities. They served as priests in their religions and ran their towns' businesses. Men were allowed an equal share in the community, with all jobs and arts open to them, and when they married, they were welcomed into their wives' homes.

Hmmm . . .

As the family sits and watches television or videos, notice how often women are victims of crimes in these shows; notice how often shows are all about "avenging" a young woman's death; notice how often women are victims who need rescuing.

Ask yourself: What are these shows teaching you to feel about yourself? If you don't like the answer, change channels, then write to the network.

Play catch with your father or uncle or brother or mother or aunt or sister.

When your father (or mother) goes out to the garage to build something or fix the car, go with him (or her) and learn.

Take your dad fishing.

Set aside an afternoon when you and your dad or a brother or uncle cook dinner together for the family.

Gloria Steinem

Could she be your hero?

Gloria Steinem spent most of her teen years caring for her clinically depressed mother. She shopped, cooked, and cleaned house, so she learned at an early age what a job it is to run a household. As an adult, she has worked to change laws and to change society so that women who work at home, as well as women who work out of the home, get fair treatment.

Help with the yard work.

Never say, "She doesn't work" about an at-home mother or wife. Say, "She works at home" instead.

Go golfing with your dad, hiking with your mom. Or vice versa.

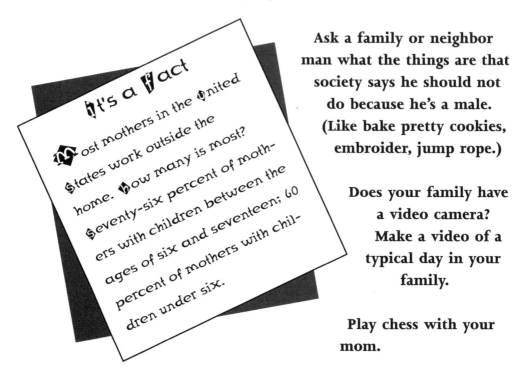

It's a Fact

Most mothers in the United States work outside the home. How many is most? Seventy-six percent of mothers with children between the ages of six and seventeen; 60 percent of mothers with children under six.

Ask a family or neighbor man what the things are that society says he should not do because he's a male. (Like bake pretty cookies, embroider, jump rope.)

Does your family have a video camera? Make a video of a typical day in your family.

Play chess with your mom.

Notice who drives your family car. And consider this: The one who drives is in charge.

Take out the garbage.

Explore your maternal ancestors. Ask your grandmother about her mother and her mother's mother. You are the descendant of many strong women.

Hmmm . . .

A recent study showed that at the family dinner table, boys get more attention than girls. They talk more and are listened to more. Girls talk less and are interrupted more. See who is getting the respect and attention at your house; discuss this with your parents; suggest some changes.

We don't see things as they are, we see them as we are.
—Anaïs Nin (writer)

my own ideas about adults

_____

_____

_____

_____

_____

_____

_____

_____

_____

_____

Women have a long, powerful history of strength and endurance. Women walked the tundra and savannas of prehistoric continents. Women developed agriculture to feed their families and mathematics to keep track of their cycles.

In ancient European societies, many gods were female; women inherited property from their mothers and passed it down to their daughters. And when these early civilizations were conquered by patriarchal (male-run) civilizations, women still miraculously survived, serving as elders in their villages, as healers to family and community, and as counselors to all.

Women ran countries—Melisend of Jerusalem (1105–1160), Eleanor of Aquitaine (1122–1202), and Margaret of Scandinavia (1353–1412), among them. A woman (Queen Isabella) was responsible for Columbus's voyage to the Americas. Women served as respected physicians. An eleventh-century woman, Trotula, wrote the book that was the doctors' guidebook to women's diseases for 700 years. Women were missionaries and abbesses, war leaders and poets. Their stories come down to us through history, stories of women who, against all odds, became renowned scientists, mathematicians, artists, and powerful leaders.

Though the lives of almost all women were limited by the rules of their societies and religions, women survived. Women continued to lobby and battle for their rights to wealth and education. And for the rights of their daughters. In the United States, in the late 1700s, when critics called educated women "unfeminine monsters," women held firm to their goals.

Women pushed for their equal rights to education and to the fruits of their labor. In England, Mary Wollstonecraft wrote *A Vindication of the Rights of Woman* (1792). In the United States, Abigail Adams warned her husband, future president John Adams, that the ladies would rebel and would not feel bound to a Constitution that did not include them.

In 1848, feminists met in Seneca Falls, New York, and the women's movement was officially launched. Women then fought a long battle for basic rights to property, education, and freedom until finally winning the right to vote seventy-two years later, in 1920. And then most women relaxed, but a few continued to work, fighting for women's rights to enter universities and businesses and to control their lives. The women's movement resurfaced again in the 1970s. Gloria Steinem and Betty Friedan and others spoke to the nation, demanding equal pay for equal work and the right to equal education.

So when people say women are fragile, that women cannot last the distance, that women are too weak for competition, think back to your history. Think back to the history of women who never gave up, not through the dark ages, not through the long, dull centuries of toil. Women have never given up; women have continued to fight for equality—sometimes quietly, sometimes loudly, but always, steadily. That is power, and that is strength, and that is feminism.

Remember "Sugar and spice and everything nice, that's what little girls are made of"? Remember people once believed this? Now think about what people believe today. Prepare to change their minds.

When you start to say about a baby girl, "Oooh, how sweet and pretty she looks," try saying, "Oooh, how strong and smart she is" instead.

When referring to a male head of a committee, call him chairperson. Do the same for women.

Listen to the words sung by your favorite music group. If they are insulting to women, find another favorite.

Oh Yeah???

Here are the facts for the next time you hear the one about girls being fragile flowers: The female body is designed for endurance and survival. Females endure the strain of childbirth but also do well and often come in first in long-distance sporting events like 100-mile runs and long-distance ocean swimming. Girls are also less vulnerable than boys to colds, flus, and infections. And female babies are less fearful than males and cry less often.

What part of "NO" don't you understand?

Think of what the world would be like if we replaced the cliché "It's a man's world" with "It's a woman's world."

For Halloween, dress up as Superman or Batman or another male hero. If people can't tell you're a girl, do they treat you differently?

It's A Woman's World

Find a video game in which a female warrior is the main character. Play that one instead of the typical old ones with male characters fighting each other for the prize at the end—treasure or a princess. If you can't find a strong female game, complain to the companies that make video games.

When men or women ridicule a woman because she is strong or outspoken—like Hillary Rodham Clinton or Gloria Steinem—stand up for the woman's right to be in charge and to have opinions.

Write to the editors of teen-oriented magazines that feature skinny, starving models. Tell them you're going to stop reading their magazines unless they start showing clothing on more realistic models.

It's a Fact

In 1995, the Feminist Majority Foundation discovered that once people know the definition of "feminism," 71 percent of females and 61 percent of males say they are feminists. That definition? A feminist is "someone who supports political, economic, and social equality for women."

Change the word "mankind" to "womankind" when reading. Notice how that feels.

Create your own vision of a strong, intelligent, satisfied woman. Draw a picture of her or find a magazine photo that reflects her. Hang it in your room to remind you.

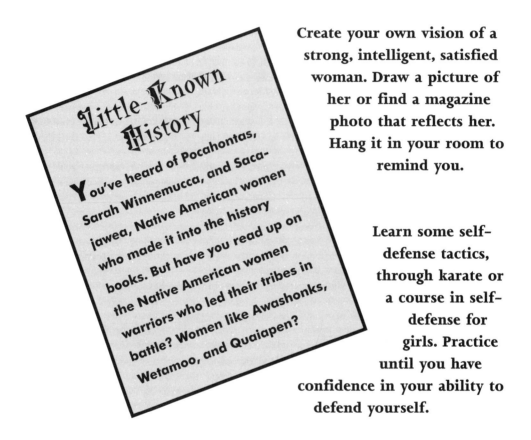

Little-Known History

You've heard of Pocahontas, Sarah Winnemucca, and Sacajawea, Native American women who made it into the history books. But have you read up on the Native American women warriors who led their tribes in battle? Women like Awashonks, Wetamoo, and Quaiapen?

Learn some self-defense tactics, through karate or a course in self-defense for girls. Practice until you have confidence in your ability to defend yourself.

Wear a feminist slogan for a day. Note the reactions of everyone to the slogan. **Sample slogan:** *Feminism is the radical notion that women are people.*

ON A SERIOUS NOTE

You will hear girls called many words that are demeaning, including ridiculous words like "chick," "broad," and "tomato." If you protest, people (even some women!) will say you are being too sensitive or that you have no sense of humor.

Protest anyway. These words are like erosion. They work, inch by inch, to dig away at a girl's self-esteem until one day she really does begin to see herself as a foolish, inferior chick.

The next time you're reading a book with a great male hero, change the "he" to "she" and the hero's name to a female name. Read it that way instead.

Little-Known History

American society has very changeable ideas about women:

1700s woman was seen as weak in intellect and moral character. Men believed they must control a woman's and family's morals.

1800s woman was seen as strong in moral character. She was the center of a family's morals and responsible for controlling a man's morals.

Today's woman is seen as a fellow human, with varying degrees of intellect and moral character. But still, a double standard exists. We are more forgiving of men's moral failings than of women's.

In the twenty-first century, what will woman be? She'll be your creation.

Keep a journal of the sexism you see in your daily life. Include your thoughts on how you could change these things.

Remember: You have a long, feminist history, and you are not a victim.

The choices we make daily for freedom in our individual lives
shape our whole society.
—Patricia Ireland (president of NOW,
the National Organization for Women)

my feminist thoughts and plans

_____

_____

_____

_____

_____

_____

_____

_____

_____

_____

get informed—
get involved

Want to learn more about the subjects we discussed in *Girl Talk*? Here's a list of organizations and associations, publications, and hotlines that are here to help you on your own unique path to shaping your world.

organizations and associations

Amateur Athletic Union

c/o The Walt Disney World Resort

P.O. Box 10,000

Lake Buena Vista, FL 32830-1000

800-AAU-4USA

Contact this organization to find out about a variety of sports teams you can join. For girls, they include basketball, baseball, volleyball, track and field, swimming, tennis, field hockey, martial arts, bodybuilding, golf, gymnastics, tumbling, in-line hockey, wrestling, aerobics, noncontact rugby, and others.

American Association of University Women (AAUW)

1111 Sixteenth Street, NW

Washington, DC 20036-4873

202-789-7700

Web site: http://www.aauw.org

E-mail: webmaster@mail.aauw.org

The AAUW sponsors and publishes many national studies about problems girls face in school. It also has many local programs to help girls do well in math and school. Contact the association to learn more.

American Youth Soccer Organization (AYSO)

5403 West 138th Street
Hawthorne, CA 90250
800-USA-AYSO
Web site: http://www.ayso.org—or—http://www.soccer.org
E-mail: webmaster@ayso.org

Contact the AYSO for teams in your area.

Association for Women in Science

1200 New York Avenue, NW, Suite 650
Washington, DC 20005
800-886-AWIS
Web site: http://www.awis.org
E-mail: awis@awis.org

This association has many local conferences and mentoring programs. Contact it for information about programs in your area.

Boys and Girls Clubs of America

1230 West Peachtree Street, NW
Atlanta, GA 30309-3447
404-815-5700

Bonnie Raitt helps to sponsor a guitar lesson program through the Boys and Girls Clubs. Call or write to this organization to find out about all the community programs in your area, from sports to homework help.

Camp Fire, Inc.
4601 Madison Avenue
Kansas City, MO 64112-1278
816-756-1950
Web site: http://www.campfire.org

Camp Fire organizes group activities for girls and boys, with focus on self-reliance and the outdoors. The Missouri headquarters will give you the name of your local Camp Fire group.

Center for the American Woman and Politics (CAWP)
90 Clifton Avenue
Rutgers University
New Brunswick, NJ 08901
908-828-2210
Web site: http://www.rci.rutgers.edu/~cawp

Go to CAWP's Web site for details on women politicians such as how many are in the U.S. Congress and who they are.

Clowns of America International (COAI)
P.O. Box 570
Lake Jackson, TX 77566
Web site: http://www.clown.org

Visit COAI's Web site or write for more information on clowns and clowning.

The Feminist Majority

1600 Wilson Boulevard, Suite 801

Arlington, VA 22209

703-522-2214

Web site: http://www.feminist.org

E-mail: femmaj@feminist.org

Contact the Feminist Majority for information on today's politics and women's status. Ask about its student internship program.

4-H Council

7100 Connecticut Avenue

Chevy Chase, MD 20815

301-961-2840

Web site: http://www.fourhcouncil.edu

The 4-H is well-known for its livestock program. If you love raising animals, contact the 4-H.

Girl Scouts of the U.S.A.

420 Fifth Avenue

New York, NY 10018-2798

212-852-8000

Web site: http://www.gsusa.org

E-mail: admin@bbs.gsusa.org

Girl Scout troops offer both indoor and outdoor activities, and a place to make friends. Contact the New York headquarters for information on a troop near you.

Girls Inc.

30 East Thirty-third Street
New York, NY 10016-5394
212-689-3700
317-634-7546 (for affiliate nearest you)
E-mail: hn3578@handsnet.org

Girls Inc. promotes better understanding for girls in math, science, and fosters self-esteem and confidence. Contact the organization for information about its programs.

International Center for Research on Women (ICRW)

1717 Massachusetts Avenue, NW
Washington, DC 20036
202-797-0007
Web site: http://www.icrw.org
E-mail: icrw@igc.apc.org

Contact this organization for information on women throughout the world.

Junior Achievement, Inc.
One Education Way
Colorado Springs, CO 80906
719-540-8000
Web site: http://www.ja.org
E-mail: webmaster@ja.org

Interested in business? Junior Achievement's slogan is "Teaching Kids How Business Works." It has programs in economics, business, and the international marketplace.

Little League
P.O. Box 3485
Williamsport, PA 17701
717-326-1921

Little League includes girls on both baseball and softball teams.

National Organization for Women (NOW)
1000 Sixteenth Street, N.W.
Washington, D.C. 20036
202-331-0066
Web site: http://www.now.org
E-mail: now@now.org

NOW is the largest feminist organization in the United States. Contact

NOW for information about today's struggle for women's equality and look for its Young Feminist events.

National Teenage Republican Headquarters

P.O. Box 1896

Manassas, VA 20108-1896

703-368-4214

Web site: http://www.rnc.org

Through this organization, you can learn more about the Republican Party and get involved in politics.

Take Our Daughters To Work Day
Ms. Foundation for Women

120 Wall Street, Thirty-third Floor

New York, NY 10005

800-676-7780

Web site: http://www.ms.foundation.org

In addition to its popular "Take Our Daughters To Work Day," the Ms. Foundation holds annual sweepstakes drawings for girls. Visit its Web site or call the toll-free number to find out more about these.

Women and Mathematics Education

c/o Charlene Morrow
Mount Holyoke College
302 Shattuck Hall
South Hadley, MA 01075
413-538-2608
E-mail: cmorrow@mhc.mtholyoke.edu

Contact this group to find out about summer math study programs.

Women in Math

University of Maryland
College Park, MD
Web site: http://www.cs.umd.edu/~gibson/wim.html
E-mail: wim@math.umd.edu

Look up this group to learn about your math opportunities. Also, see its Web site for biographies of women in math, and Web links to sites in science, engineering, and computing.

Young Democrats
Democratic National Committee

430 South Capitol Street, SE
Washington, DC 20003
202-863-8000

Web site: http://www.democrats.org

E-mail: dnc@democrats.org

Contact this group to find out more about the Democratic Party and about how you can get involved in politics.

YWCA (Young Women's Christian Association)

726 Broadway

New York, NY 10003

212-614-2700

E-mail: hn2062@handsnet.org

Contact the YWCA for after-school programs and sports programs.

on the web

Share ideas and your own humorous outlook on life with other girls. Find girls' Web clubhouses like the one at http://www.agirlsworld.com, where girls share jokes, their thoughts, craft ideas, and information about famous women. The Web is growing and changing all of the time, so if this site or another site is not there when you call it up, go to one of your favorite girls' Web pages and look for links. Girls love to share ideas, and they're sharing them on the Web. Join in.

Also, are you excited about the ideas and information you have found in *Girl Talk*? Or do you have some that you would like to add? Send your comments and thoughts to the author, Judith Harlan, at her E-mail address: jharlan@west.net—She would love to hear from you.

publications

Girls' Life

4517 Harford Road
Baltimore, MD 21214
410-254-9200

This magazine, for girls between the ages of seven and fourteen, has stories about everything in a young girl's life. It talks about outdoor events and indoor crafts, about parties and friends. And it includes stories and info about real girls, not just famous people.

New Girls Times

215 West Eighty-fourth Street
New York, NY 10024
212-873-2132
E-mail: nugrltim@aol.com

The New Girls Times bills itself as "the only national newspaper written by girls." It runs about eight to twelve pages and is upbeat, with articles exploring such subjects as what it is like being smart and being a girl, cen-

sorship and dress codes in school, and girls who start their own businesses.

New Moon
The Magazine for Girls and Their Dreams
P.O. Box 3620
Duluth, MN 55803-3620
218-728-5507
Web site: http://www.newmoon.org

A girls' editorial board oversees this magazine and publishes articles about women and girls all around the world—for girls from eight to fourteen years old. Read this magazine to help build your confidence and self-esteem, as well as to learn about women's values. Also, visit the New Moon Web site to see a sampling of the magazine and to share your ideas with the girls there.

Wahine
5520 East Second Street, Suite K
Long Beach, CA 90803
310-434-9444
E-mail: Wahinemag@aol.com

A magazine for women and girls who love the water, Wahine focuses on women's surfing, bodyboarding, and other ocean sports. Even if you're not a surfer, you'll enjoy the magazine's athletic attitude.

Women's Sports + Fitness
170 East Sixty-first Street, Sixth Floor
New York, NY 10021
212-980-5580

This is the official magazine of the Women's Sports Foundation, and though it is for adult women, you'll find some inspiring articles in here about today's female athletes—runners, bikers, climbers, ballplayers.

other magazines

There's a magazine for every interest. Think of what you like to do—from in-line skating, to swimming, reading, collecting rocks, to anything you can think of. Find the magazines that cover the subjects you care about. Notice how many women are writers on the magazines and how many are included in the stories. If these numbers are too low for a given magazine, call or write to the magazine and tell the editor about it. The customer is always right, and you are the customer.

Many magazines have Web sites, too, which give you a sample of the 'zines' attitudes and articles. Always use caution and smarts when on the Web, but surf it to check out 'zines on the topics that interest you.

hotlines

American Anorexia/Bulimia Association

293 Central Park West, #1R
New York, NY 10024
212-501-8351

Phone or write to this association for information about eating disorders and for the name of a local group that can help.

Boys Town National Hotline

800-448-3000

Although this is called "Boys Town," it is a twenty-four-hour hotline for all kids and parents. Call for advice on any serious concern or problem.

The National Domestic Violence Hotline

800-799-7233 (800-799-SAFE)

If you are concerned that a friend or family member may be a victim of domestic violence, or if you are one yourself, call this hotline for advice.

National Youth Crisis Hotline

800-442-4673

Call this number anytime, for help with any crisis, from family violence to personal problems. The hotline can also help you get away from gangs, drugs, alcohol, or other outside pressures.

Youth Crisis Hotline

800-448-4663

This twenty-four-hour hotline provides help with any crisis and tells you where to go for further help in your area.

runaway hotlines

Covenant House 9-Line: 800-999-9999
National Runaway Switchboard: 800-621-4000

If you know someone who is a runaway, or if you have left home yourself or are thinking of doing so, call either of these numbers for help—for messages, shelter, or advice.

index